A FIELD AT VALLORCINES

GW00801782

A Field at Vallorcines

ROLAND MATHIAS

First Impression—October 1996

ISBN 1 85902 304 5

© Roland Mathias

This volume is published with the support of the Arts Council of Wales.

Printed in Wales at
Gomer Press, Llandysul, Ceredigion.

CONTENTS

ONSET OF WINTER

A thin cataract
Across the mountain's eye
Before the oak
Flocks its last leaves.
Patches of snow attempt the look
Of rigour, hardily
Swearing winter will make it fact.

And the air sharply swears
There shall be no sap
Unfrozen in stem
Or footstep, leave
What you will in dish or crumb
Defiantly. Gossip
Hobbles along with what appears.

But for all the miss
In the steady beat
Of the walking blood
Stopped at the bark
The lamed man keeps his heat
Aware, like the cold, shut clod,
An ancienter oath will answer this.

ABER

Is there a bearing to this spot
From where she rises, limned, beyond
The distant stands of light? Or is it not
Permitted, the occasional fond

Recollection, the hastily scribbled note
Of a name, of where the body is
In the black pen-umbraed mass? Such anecdote
As I have requires the emphasis

Of this tumbled close, the tossing waste
Of hill, the sombre rain coming on
At tea-time. No quicker motion, not even haste
Of words need leap to show. The one

To tell where I've been to, how the dull
Affection aches, quick spine just sensed
Alive in this yard, though drawn straight from the coil
Of wounds, struck free and audienced.

I have no prayers like hers, that sprang
Hard from the laid-down rock, but now,
All lenient muscles tensed, I'll practise long
After dark, if she remember too.

TŶ CLYD

A fortnight has gone since her death.
February hangs browned at the edge
Like the snowdrop's sheath.
If there is life still, low in the old drudge
Garden, its crying virtue belongs
With the ground wind, with the weary pokings
At door-jambs, the shuddered gravel
Dry-soled, back and fore, bleak with conscience left behind.

The staid house looks hard at the town,
Elbowed and spry as the hills
Completing the frown.
Builder Meredith capped it, the bills
Depressed by his weight, the deeds held by
Six-foot-six Wilcockson, daily
The Bulwark's barber. O unapt,
It was first dubbed 'The Olives' in the town rate book.

But that day the bluff dead were young,
Sprigs like the house. Dapper world.
David Morgan not long
The rich draper, Arafnah Thomas called
To be minister, booked for the greater fuss
Of marrying his daughter. Part of that choice
Was the house, whether to have
Or to let to a bank-clerk, who cut the new Welsh on the door.

But for thirty-nine narrowing years
My mother it was kept the house
Squared at its peers.
In the master-bedroom the ceiling throws
Off the hills' pale blue: that shade would rouse
Low light awake in the burned-out hollows
Of my father's failing eye, like some
Onset of song near dark, the nightingale returned.

9

Cosy was rarely its state
Over decades of waiting when *clyd*
White-lettered the gate.
Principled rather, two storeys of deed
Slapped on word, a house with all chance crusades
Abandoned, a crux of definitive shades
Attacking the quiet. Graver
My business when I am hidden from its looks.

THE STEWARD'S LETTER

To the Lo. Burghley

Right hon^{or}able
My humble dewtie holden
In minde, please to be adv^{er}tized that yor
Comaund nowe restes secured
In maner folowinge:

It is not easie
To keepe the dead in w^{or}shippe
Who have beene marked by follie in the^r lives
But what the formes demaund
Has beene fulfiled f^r yor late couzen
William, lest the publicke weale
Dissolve imediatelie in sland^{er}
Or that what is yor hon^{or}s dewe
Tumble with^t wille or reputacon
Into anoth^{er}s hande.

Bef^{or}e the coffyn
Wente vi poore men the p^{ar}ishe
Caste as worthie, gowned in suche stuffe of blacke
As suites yor griefe, Herefordes
Prebent nexte, gravelie acompanyed
Wth my uncle P^{ar}ry, yor couzens
Late wifes broth^{er}. Rude scutcheninges
Of Cicilles, P^{ar}rys and H^{ar}batts armes
I had hadde stitched to the coffyn clothe, and
Cladde in wholesome blacke

Vi of my fath^{er}
In lawes mens^{ar}vauntes b^{or}e him
To Churche y^{ar}de, whence from the Churche do^{or} in
Of his viii sonning lawes
In murninge clocks and answerable

11

Apparel vi bore him on. Three
Nephewes in licke sorte folowed
Aft^{er}, yor couzens sister Ales
In murninge gowne and in licke atyer
Viii doughters folowinge.

I had the nave walles
Hanged all wth blacke and aft^{er}
Suche concourse as the Church c^d not conteyne
Had part dispersed a dole,
Two penn^{orth} of bread and monie both,
The poore attendinge had, the^{ir}
Number more thanne iv hundred.
And the nexte day anoth^{er} dole
Of halfe as muche a hundred persons
Poore of this p^{ar}ishe each

Had as his dewe. In
Man^{er} so the funeralls
Were compleated, and that the credit might
Attache to yor couzens howse
Of Alterinis I gave oute
The charge to bee yor Lo:shippes,
All of a hundred pownds and uppwardes
As by p^{ar}ticul^{ar}s shalbe shortely
Manifeste. Thus to yor comendacon
Was this s^{ar}vice donne.

But it consorted
Ille that Mawde, yor couzens
Wife now livinge, albeit requested, sawe
Fitte not to come, the clothe
Of blacke sent to h^{er} roome returned
In silence. Also that Mathew,
My fath^{er} in lawes sowle hyer, childeles
And unfitted in minde f^r pref^{er}ment,
Throwe wekenes and sinist^{er} councell yet allowes
Not his fath^{er}s wille

Is ille enowe f^{r}
O^{r} peace. Yet in the writinge
I doe but keepe backe worse, so much dismayed
Am I f^{r} the int^{er}este
Yo^{r} hon^{or} has in these Cicill landes.
A bonde nowe f^{or}fayte falleth dewe
By Powell of Llansoy, atte one
Tyme s^{ar}vaunt to her maiestie,
Uppon his fayly^{er} to deliver a rente
On average 80 powndes

Yearlie, the dowry
His moth^{er} should have gotten
In m^{ar}ying yor late couzen William.
Withal that moth^{er} fulle
Of ranc^{or} latelie has conveyed
Plate worthe a hundred markes
To the selfsame Powell, parte
Being the cuppe of silv^{er} and giltte that was
Yo^{r} hon^{or}s gifte to my late mast^{er}
As well to defray the charge

Of the funerall doles, as
To yelde some comforte unto
Yo^{r} late couzens children. Sithens I am
Enformed the said Powell lyes
Abedde and dangerouslie sicke
Wee are licke to have this dette
And muche els f^{or}fayt. I doe beseche
Yo^{r} hon^{or} makke me a grante of w^{ar}dshippe
Of Powells hyer, his broth^{er} Symonds
Sonne, that haplie wee

May repayre the fortunes
Of the howse conformable to
Yo^{r} hon^{or}s name and reputacon.
My broth^{er} Mathew lyeth

Sicke of the t^{ar}magauntes and licke
To dye.

Thus I comitte yor
Lo:shippe to the almighties care
This xiiith day of Marche. From my howse
At Preston uppon Wye. Yo^{r} humble
To comaund, Paul Delahay.

THE PATH TO FONTANA AMOROSA

Take this cliff path, no other, let your eye
Wind between sea and flower. It is all
Magic. Cistus and cistus blush
For their mountaining sisters, cyclamen
Flaunting a pallor more chaste are just
Out of the reach. Scent follows ravening scent
To the ultramarine. What does it matter
If Ariosto was never here in the flesh
For all his lushness? Sufficient it was
To know this the white goddess's country,
All the elate ten miles of it, carob
And fig-tree and myrtle, tauntingly to the spring
Where the gush is all women's abandon, the stone
Cloak falling from the pale world's beautiful.
Can it be less than magic as the reckless coast
Unfolds? Conspiracy winking off each blue
Sea-hood's shoulder, each craggier rock
Diverts the step with quickening talk of Akamas,
His wedding to the incandescent slip
Of a girl whose fountain plays ahead. But look
There! Burnet spines are pitting the cistus
Faces, the amorous cliff recedes. By that
Extravagant boulder a lizard big enough
To have known better lies no more
Than bloat. The snake's repellent hiss
Comes back from a sidling crack in the stone.
There is one quick lover the less. Why do you falter
Half a mile on and defer to reach
That legendary fountain? Is your return
Confirmed by the carcases, lizard and snake
Flayed both by a happened wheel since the leap
Of your passing? Onasias, who honoured his father
And mother twenty-five hundred years ago
In Marion, he had this path to take
Or not to take, these blazing flowers

To pick, this shore to travel. But how
To consult such a spirit? Polis, the odd
Vestigial city from which you must
Set out, separates boast from arrival,
The live from the few loving dead. Eucalyptus
Trees, a grove half skirted with bamboo eyots
Cursed in with gravel and sea-water,
Quiver where Marion was. That speaking grave
For all you know despairs with its words
Awash. Whose country it is as the child days
Vanish, stranger, has more to decide than you.

INNOCENT DYING

Grey is Nant Iago, grey
With slate planes and break-offs
From the darker roughs
Shot dead in the mines on Cedris. They

Lie flat now, assembled, flat
As the lives of old miners.
Calms immerse
Them, hold them in a cold mercy, set

Grey in their faces, grey
Run weedless, the surface
Clean. It is
Only a skate now to confluence, shy

Death in Dysynni, death
By confusion. Close by at
This gorsy spit
You can see the swathe of green weed beneath

The wave of Dysynni, wave
Going humped with the fields' knap
That's higher up.
A step further shows you Iago, grave

And resistless, hand
His cap in, simple
With years. The full
River swills undyed from his token end.

SIGNAL

The corner of an eye pricks
Me. A change? What has happened
Is just out of sight but touching
Somehow, touching. I turn
And catch a leaf in flight
From the wisteria, orange–
Yellow, afloat
In a totally familiar silence.
It parachutes slowly to its far ground
Undeviating, already remote.

Whatever stance I take
There is another in the eye's
Corner and, reckless, another,
Another. Their first take-off
Is secret, and what beck
They jump to who knows either?
I sense no wind.
Must I ghost them downward, follow
Their course to the markers set
For yellow, sudden but disciplined.

EXPIATION

I called you cringer, grandfather
Whom I never knew, chooser
Among the aliens. I hedged
The glats to the east of the old
Coedcae, set it at prouder
Slope, recalled it stood leased
From Wales.

But other tales were forgotten, how
At the fairground, stripped, you took
The booth professional
Slam-bang in the second, rather
In duty to mates than fury
Of blood, since you had reckoned
Cardiff

A kick-off for a builder of sorts.
But muscle treated for allies
Briefly. The bouts you lost
Were with coughing, never the pick
Of antagonists. Uphill
The wiseacres gestured, to savour
Banu's

Air. But whose is the choice after
The gullet half-chokes with fears?
Hunching over the fire
You saw your death in a chute
Of ash and cried out louder
Than any comfort. Beneath
Twyn Du

You lie. It is useless to say I am
Sorry. Yours was another
World, its rages all mould
In the present. But to deny
The dead a voice is to falter
In justice. Whatever it meant
Ffynnon

Fawr got me born, and what marks it now
Is the one dark tree you planted
Hard by the quivering
Water.

SATURDAY MORNING: APPIN

Storm hit the van roof sharply after dark,
Rain far past midnight rattling on like shot.
But morning came with a calm, all the sky pale
And the paused earth hung with midges. Still
As the weave of water is and the boats
Barely at bob, no jar or slightest pull
On their lines, the picture is not quite
Mirrored. Lismore shafts into sun
In a while, its crofts barred white on the long
Green back the island makes. And the *bheinns*
Of Morven begin to shade and scale
As the cloud-rolls top and break up
From the west, staring like improbable
Giant saurians sated or not yet fully
Awake. In the quiet the foreshore brims:
The piled-up lobster-pots, the cross-braced posts
Once stanchions for a pier, the snub
White lighthouse on its braded rock
In the middle bay, recover poise
After hours of beating. Sad that the heart
Comes back more slowly, peers away
From the flattened sea-loch out to the hairline
Threat of ocean, its ear of blood still cocked
For uneasy combers wickedly raking
A far-off western head that has been
Fixed ever since that fainter coast was laid.

THEY, WITHOUT US*

'Voices are voices, when all's said.
Don't witter on about "an urgent tone".
They're soldiers stumping down there on the plat
Where the field edge breaks and before
That river bend winds in. You cock
That ear for no ostensible reason, Crwys.
This is a civilised country.

I don't understand your interest, man.
Let's talk about something else. That trip
To the Gower you were rabbiting on about
For Sunday. All the aqua gear to take
And Baldwin to let know. But Barbarossa not.
Wastes our time with his birds, he does.
The sport's the thing, after all.

They're sure to show up in a minute
Crossing Llangynidr Bridge. For heaven's sake,
Crwys, what's it to us? Some short route march
From Cwrt-y-Gollen probably, poor silly
Buggers that went for soldiers, sweating
Their follies out. I'm all for doing
What I want, no harm to others.

What's this you're muttering? Soldiers never
March up a river bank? And Cynog, damn,
Who's he? Thomas Coke, Carnhuanawc, Roger Price? Not
Even names to me. Your lips are white,
Boy, take hold that post a minute. We'll
See them swinging as they cross. What *does*
It matter if they see *us*?'

---

* 'God having provided some better thing for us, that they, without us,
should not be made perfect.' (Hebrews 11:40)

22

CYNOG

And from which mountain
Did the bald hermit fall? Fan
Oleu or the greater Fan
Where the camp of the iron users was?

At stake is benison
Not history. Which horn
Of Yscir benefits? What crown
Succeeds the boar, stag, fish and the treeful

Of bees that Drichan
Blessed? For they strained and shone,
All four of them, brilliant on
The links of the golden collar

Giraldus was shown
A moment, that Brychan
Set on the dandled infant when
He was brought back muling to the king's

Garthmadryn, the son
Of violation
Decorated. But why enjoin
More mystery? The child in the midst

Of his kin made on
Towards manhood, but unknown
To the chroniclers. The vital one
Conundrum the mountainheads keep to

Themselves, cordon
Like conscience. Five decades on
When raiders came whose pagan
Screams, back winded, had carried too faint

To Uther's column
Flummoxed in darkness upon
Wyebank, no kneeling deacon
Could interpose or cry panic

To the dark farms. In
The osier hut he lay prone
On rags, the startling burden
Of collar hidden under his

Bulking robe. Alien
Howls broke in, a train
Of flame spat out osiers, then
Execration burned in a score

Of voices. More than
One look at the stiff old man
Was witless. To the cliff with the Christian
Skullhead and fire to his lurking

God. Cynog, waxen,
Travelled in silence, a wan
Blessing falling with him. When
Did the true soul go without company?

I stand convinced on
The outer mound of the iron
Users' camp, perhaps mistaken
But unconfronted by adversaries,

Pursuing benison
Down past lichened trees, sodden
Leaves on projecting ledges, on
To the hurtling blur of winter deeps,

Believing ruffian
Ends are baffled, that down
In Yscir the fish breathes patiently in
The river's turbulence and of late

Alder boughs have been
Swarmed by a hive again
Of native bees. Of the hidden
Collar two parts are back in place

And two are stolen.
In this veiled afternoon
By the bed of a pagan autumn
There is time for a holy silence.

TERNS AT ROSSNASKILL

Whiter than sand
Is white between
The rock talons brandishing
This promontoried strand
The terns loop, elegant,
Lean, the sea's white
Swallows, embroidering
Up-wind and down the damascene
Showcloth that bright
Evening runs up the lidless
Window. Noonlight
Skies have no such spare
Nonchalance as this.
Down-turned the angled
Bone, the pattern is
Careless, air itself
Has bravado, leaping bare
From such wings
To fresh platforms of height.

The terns banking, cruising,
Occasional raucous
Blasts on their intercom,
Tingle the nerve in us
Of distant war, a shoal
Of kernes in another hemisphere
Marked down for slaughter.
In the rippled fathom near
Black-headed divers already
At work advance the cull
By a minute before the definitive
Stoop begins. It is queer,
This standing within
The envelope, pulse
Beating quicker, while sand,

Rock and all else
Quiver like vertebrates
Caught without hope or luck
By the hundred thousand.

All of a sudden
The first loop breaks. One
Of the terns, not
Having cast so much as a look
From the slit eye over
The hooked, arrogant beak,
Stoops as no pilot does, short
Like a stone to the slack
Between ripples, cutting
The divers apart, a blade-bone
Cleaving the wavelets'
Interface. We distinguish
No victim, though not
Doubting there is one.
An undulation of whites
Marks the ruttish
Inelegance instinct calls
To such rites. As the tern
Angles his wings and kneels
Before take-off, a victor
Making oblation, a poor sort
Of life is conferred
On the scourings, a few short
Minutes for turmoil. Now
As the ripples go over
The mackerel shoal, nothing
Is lost but one pale
Out of the shallows myrmidon.

ON DISCOVERING DAUMIER'S 'DON QUIXOTE READING' IN THE NATIONAL MUSEUM AT CARDIFF

It should have been no surprise,
Quixote, this corner turned,
To encounter you burning quietly
As Beltenebros, fitting those
Slashed, interminable bones
With a chary flesh, a faint
New rosy scarring pricked in
By recent dreams. You are back
At your beginning, the book
A refresher course with Amadis
Of Gaul and the other mad
Celts your masters. Old tilts
Are overlaid, Rocinante stalled
At the *Neue Pinakothek,* lean
With comparisons. Nothing
Compels these Iron Age legs
Crossed in the hour of this
Visit but that multi-printed horizon
Where a hundred ills disperse
Barely audible cries of anger
Or distress. You are a skull
Driven by story and the centuries
Of man. It is you who call up
The Lord of Taprobane in a sierra
Dust-cloud, though the Summer Country
Has dried in the leaguered heat
Of Christendom. Illiterate
Dulcinea is no more than
A point of reference on your map
Of charges, inked up with ridicule
And the odd splat of blood. Yet
Those bones twitch from grave

To grave, updating the cerements.
I know when
I turn the corner next
You'll have been long in this dark
And gone.

A FIELD AT VALLORCINES

Drops of the rain that tumbled the runnels
Half an hour ago forbodingly hang
From the under-bars of the seat. But abundantly plain

It is that the mountainy drapes so long
Clambered through cannot well be defied
Here where the field cries halt. We can sit and count

The unchemicalled flowers, the red ambuscade
Of clover, the dandelions tall as the grasses
And sorrel policing the burley. For this lush field

Is past season too, the goalpost crosses
Rear woodenly out of the herbage, remember
The game as it was. Away to the left a few

Conifers, planted singly, sombre
The path we took this morning. It
Entices still, its winding masters the slant

Of the brow to the massier trees despite
That knowledge we have of rain. A charm
It has, and promise, and the col above is no less

For the cold of hearts on arrival. Storm
Passes by, flags other, distant alps,
Falls quiet. It is calm here. On the old

Hindmost rushes water gulps
Out jewels and the seep of the field
Is audible. To the right the fenced way pushes

Past garden palings and partly tilled
Vegetable plots to the railway line
Beyond. But the station building, the immediate goal,

Has a kind of grace, a fluted, fine
Semblance of gothic tricked into the metal.
The run down the gorge to the frontier, the silent place

We peered at this morning with so little
In mind, will be full of jerks and slowings
Like the blind climb up. But the station has grace. It has borne

The faces of doubt, the comings and goings
Of millions. We shall stand there solid in
The goodly counsel with which a world back we set out.

ON SOUTH LORD'S LAND

On South Lord's Land
Water is slippery
Suddenly, chalybeate,
Staining occasional
Limestone edges dark
Gamboge. This gill drops
Quickly from mind, like
A friend gone off
To the enemy, only
To morse in with chuck
And plop and frank moss
Mischiefed and shot
Garnet-dull as rock.
Whether single or double
Agent this slip means
To try the beaked gardes
Of this bogland, letting go
The patient crannies of origin.
Stop here: these veins
From the past are narrowing:
Only twists of water
Escape. When the Raven
Signals gutter, best we are
Covert allies of Owain's
Or frowsty camp-followers
Not unexpected in Rheged.

SANDERLINGS

That plump little chorus
Tripping balletically,
Leaning delicately into the gale
With the daft precision
Of a collective toy,
Was wound up with a skein
From the ice-cap. This
Is the rude Ardudwy
Station: some skill in
Diplomacy compels
These spasms of wittering,
The tiny side-stepping
Runs that carry the watcher
From foam to deliquescent
Foam and no further, since
The wind postpones take-off
And the chorus ticked in
At Murmansk must whir
Till the Orange River
Groans like a lighthouse
In the craw of survivors.
Naïve of us, then, to cry
Strangers: for a storm in Wales
Trims their flight, not
Their purposes, and wise
We should know whose birds
By right sing here
Before clapping these travellers
Welcome.

RONAN

Ronan
   Lofting in the brake
Scanning the sun
For recognition
   Of the Immaculate Ego
Collated by thorn
   And a scholarly
         Wind

His back
   Shut to the Menez Hom
Required the black
Wolves of the hillock
   To make his spare offering
And the few spindlestick
   Trees to sharpen
         Thoughts

He played
   Like beads along the week.
The gorse obeyed
Him, birds more afraid
   Of lightning than indignant
Harriers had cried
   His boundaries,
         Crows,

Magpies,
   Bickered beyond the cave's
Approaches, bees
Obliged with honeys
   From herbs on distant commons.
The bare hilltop was
   A discipline
         Struck

Above.
　Below in Kernévé
Wickedness drove
Young women furtive
　In untidiness, fleshly
Abandon and grave
　Labour of sons.
　　　　Men

Numbered
　Scuffles as the hit
Of their sleazy guard
On honour, toward
　Which few took a dying
Step. It was word
　Of such commonwealth
　　　　Kept

Ronan
　Abhorrent in his cave
Rapt in the mien
Of saint, an opinion
　That love was untouchable
Save for the one
　Alone in the cosmos.
　　　　Time

And no
　Tender humblings on
He stumbled, knew
He was dead. And through
　Forest bogs the bearers
Slithered, blew
　A squat trumpet.
　　　　Now

Ronan
  Buried in his shift
Could bless both kin
And kingdom, common
  As each might be. How better
To light upon
  The clearing where
    He

Should lie
  Than by asking of
The Spirit. They
Bundled the body
  Stiffening upon an ox-cart,
Whipped up the
  Oxen and let
    Them

Take their
  Churning course as they
Would. Through the briar
Thickets, the higher
  Pales of the forest the ox-cart
Smashed till the bare
  Slopes of the Menez
    Hom

Came back.
  Ronan in his shift
Raised himself, spoke
From the travelling cart-deck
  To his sleeping blood. His body
Petrified, struck
  Him a monu-
    Ment.

CAE IAGO: MAY DAY

Among these arthritic contours,
Little atlas and himalaya
Dip down to cwms of glaciered pasture
And stiffen, back to the bluff
Of a new rigidity. Most of the old
Walls have fallen, the blackthorn
Splushes have grown out, and each
Of the half enclosures has its
Happy trackway up or on behind
That outburst of rock, beyond
This bracken hill. Cock
Pheasants walk these broken
Enclosures, their picking step
Unharassed. The sheep have their
Winter coats round their ears
And the lambs making play by
Tree roots limber and jump
On each other in the brief
Seconds that sun has
To manoeuvre the clouds away.

It is all new! It is not just
Spring hiding behind the snow showers
Or the damson budding again
From its fungused bark. Over
The vanquished summits Ieuan
Appears, his big-wheeled Honda
Trike pursued by sheep, or at
Feeding time rattles a tractor
Down improbable slopes, unbagging
Beet-pulp nuts in trail along
Some shelf of grass, keeping
The hollow bricks of ochred
Minerals topped up. The old

Nomad was right. What has the air
Of cities but obstruction and
The hospital breath of in-fighting?
Up here the men are dead
Who might have argued and the world
Goes on. Snow slants between
This window and Hafotty Ganol's
Ruin across the cwm: the pheasant
Makes his parade: surviving man
Roars up the bounds of his latest kingdom.

GRASSHOPPERS

What is it to grasp,
From this moment, this hasty
Bolt of food on the Rhinerhorn
Where the wimberries thin out
And the few stunts of spruce have
Already reckoned with winter? Patently
It is the grasshoppers I
Must listen to, as they intersperse
A hard leg-music with mad
Travels from tussock to bleaker
Tuft, to broken stick or random
Protuberant stone. Some of these
Rakish frames hark back lime-
Green in talk, some converse
In brown or blue. But every one
Presently makes hard music in
A stop in this Indian summer of his,
Knowing there's no survival
Except in the eggs that instinct
Buried in the entablature àt the
Inevitable season. Rightness
Is not in question. It is plainly
Right, here where the trees
On the contour are ellipses, faint
And separate in the transverse sun
Stretching to the strict blue ridge
They will never attain, it is right
To climb as we can, to the limit
Of will. To do less
Is unworthy of such sun, such far
Blue purpose as the distance is,
Folded back and back, fainter
And fainter always, surpassing
Peak with peak, till the day
Is what we can never be and scarcely comprehend.

JAZZ FESTIVAL

What I am trying to say
Looks foolish, doesn't it,
With all this noise going on?
The town has been charmed with jazz,
Like a chameleon, putting its mouth
Just so. Have you understood
What it says?
        Each of us has ears and
Some persuasiveness. Do you think
We need such a rumpus
In the small hours of the afternoon?
Or are we slowly remembering something
Of the vainglorious shapes of riot
Which the shuffling out–island slaves
Would put on when Picton had
The reins in Trinidad.
        I cross the bridge
Leaving the town. The Usk
Is thin and willowy. The martins
Make their holes in the bank
Just as usual. Why should I listen
More fervently when the town fixes its
Walls around me, though I hear nothing
But the vexed bass?
        When I was jaunty
And unafraid, the river hill was
Dinas, staining the right bank
With shadow, canvassing the sticks
About the edge. But what is the dismal
Sum of this itinerary? Is there some
Happy issue, of the town as well
As the river? Or should it be this humbling
Bass? Could it be assumed
That time and his friends do not
Make mistakes?

THE LAMENTATION OF MARCHELL

My father, Tewdrig, has an unpromising way
With him. He thinks he knows
What the fates are and how they
Can be diverted. The sharpness coming
From the mountains strangles the ferocious
Cold here at Llanfaes, he says,
Making even a princess tremble. But I don't
Understand what the auguries can do
In this savage weather. I would rather have
The cold in the depth of my kirtle
Like a stern reproof, slowing
My blood.

My father's wish, also to be construed,
Looks to Dublin, to Aulach, with
The constraints of travel and the boorish
Hopes of arrival. But that's not how
My marriage will be decided, when the tawniness
Of osiers thicken and the princes,
Like the hazels, will find their
True vocation.

It has happened. Tarell
And Senni are iced all over.
Now I have no choice in the matter.
My father is alarmed, has three
Hundred men from the further region
Of Garthmadrin, beyond the Honddu
And the Yscir Fawr, where the great vicious
Horses are.

My trouble is easy, you will say.
Can the sons of Liathan, swarming the passes
Like ants on the stones of Maes Madoc, test
The mountain ways openly? Do you think

That the Tywi gives a huzza waiting
For my retinue to pass? Yes, there are
Messages always like fibs between
Evil and evil.

All the same, it was a fearsome night
At Glansevin, under the black combs
Of the hills. The sons of Liathan wrestled
A hundred men off the rocks. Was it
The same lank kerns who tried my ranks
At Meidrim in the last cold of the conflict?
I do not know why my step
Should be so bitter, except that my father
Wished it.

Now the auguries in the west are engrossed
And the haven of Porthmawr fits his ambition
I should be content. The rocks are smooth:
I can make my ship live, like Aulach's
In the salty tides of Dublin. The terminal
Cold has gone and my companions
Are rested. But I am distraught
Of ambition: the old heart is not with me
As it was in Garthmadrin. A feather
Will take my eye. Come, see a craning child
Wanting a toy.

THE CLEAR SEA

Brendan looked down. It was the morning of
Saint Peter the Apostle's
Day, moist, sweet-smelling, fragrant,
Almost a mouth-filling, good-looking
Day. He looked down again
To the optical deeps inert
Beneath the keel

And saw the fish there, taking the morning off
Like Saint Peter, tying their
Heads to their stirring tails. Obliging
Creatures they were, some of them tiny
Heads of phosphorus, like
Two pins on a pincushion, looking
Tidy on the sea-bottom.

But when Brendan said Mass, breaking into
The Apostle's day with
Intoning, the brothers saw the fish jeering
At them, seeking to invade like
Thin, elongated sword-fish.
How could they not see, fearing
With blunt faces,

That the cocky multitude of racy
Fishes before Brendan's
Nose, flashing with the bible in
Their mouths, would slip into nothingness
Soon, happy to reach
Out into seas dutiful, certain
There may be such?

The fishes swam in bully circles
Like the Apostle's gait
Before the host, passing wide out
Behind the man of God, as he hummed the
Sailor's tune, clement
And accurate along
The sailor's way.

But Brendan had its message straight
In the warm weather
Rejoicing, and the stirring tails are
Spread abroad, swimming paths
Of choice. All the fishes swam
Fantastic shapes there
Above in the clear sea.

LOOK AT ME, CALEB

Believe what the land is, whether
It be fat or lean.
See what woods might be on it, ilex
Or olive. This is the first sally
In our beleaguered
Stance.

I see, Caleb, and sometimes with
Oshea, that you do
Misunderstand me. When the others
Grumble at not finding water
That is their silly
Tribute

To me. Think of the children of
Anak, who have the best
Pomegranates. Do you reckon
The next grapes at sunset from
The valley of Escob
Are sour?

I speak what I believe, and
Do. It is not
Everything that the Lord knows
In his panoply of cloud.
Look at me, Caleb.
It's time.

Half a dozen poems
for the Spoon River Anthology
after Edgar Lee Masters

DR JOHN JAMES WILLIAMS

When the shepherd laid the fire
At Cwmbanu
I had begun to be weary.
The paper seemed full of court cases
And my children full of Welsh

History. It's years since I left
St. Andrews and
Became a member of the College
Of Surgeons and left off doctoring.
I lived in Mumbles, doing nothing

Except keeping the nineteenth-century
Peace. Ten years
Later my household was called
La Parisienne under a lodging-house
Keeper. But that was after I

Built Aberclydach. Then I
Was Captain of the 1st
Volunteer Battalion of the South
Wales Borderers. The rifle range at Slwch
Made my men braggers. Of course

I had the money from my
Grocer father who
Thought only of money. But
I liked to have my fill of farms
Like Elormeirch in the uplands

—And houses in Heolrhydd and
Prospect Row and
Clawygaer and Mount Street
Fields. Some of this came to me from
The railway, the Brecon and

Merthyr. I was one of the
First directors,
And of the Bargoed Coal Company.
But wouldn't it have been better in
My middle years, thinking

Of Mary and that ogre Overton,
If I had somehow
Listened to my wife and told
Her that she need not go to Clifton,
Except to see and comfort Mary.

It was no good at Paddington
And Earl's Court
That Fred and Kate and Alice
Would have me in their company. I am
A slavish fool not to enjoy

My own wife's companionship.
I was once a man
Of luxury, talking always of
Pleasing times. Now I haven't the impetus
To make my villagers talk.

When the shepherd comes to make
My fire at Cwmbanu
I have my daily paper, knowing
That half of my family hates me. Will
It be always as cruel as this?

MARY JANE ROBERTSON WILLIAMS

O Mary J.—
I didn't know that the old fellow
Would turn nasty

When we skipped
Around the shooting box.
I was the last

To go. How
Did I know my nails
Would fail me

At the last moment.
I am a childish culprit,
O Mary J.—

HOWELL PRICE WILLIAMS

I left Liverpool on the 15th
Of December 1913, on board the Blue
Funnel liner *Aeneas*. I had finished
The refurbishment of Aberclydach
House, pointed in Aberthaw ground–
Lime mortar. Notes of my journey

Through Africa made my name
In the Brecon papers. I knew my trade
As a photographer, passing old Dufile
Where Emin Pasha was made prisoner
Years ago. But, of course, my dreams

Of ground–nuts failed me
In the end. Perhaps my photograph
Did not suit me ('my little beard
Was very small') and the habit
Of playing pianola records to schoolgirls

Was not very seemly. Colonel Snead
Was my companion in Jamaica
When I took yellow fever and died there.

WILLIAM RETLAW JEFFERSON WILLIAMS

I tried being a lawyer but was
Broken down at my first defence.

Shy and retiring, I lodged at
Cross Oak House, an inn
Where I thought to have sanctuary

From my father's house. But Mrs.
Williams, who used to go huckstering

At Dowlais market, had a daughter
—A fine-looking girl—who undermined
My scattered defences. I was not

A coaxer. Why should I be? I was
Disinherited, as they say, but

Still had my twenty-five thousand
To build Brynoyre half a mile
From my father's house. I always

Despised my father's gentleman-
Like strategy in thinking himself

One of the *uchelwyr*. There was no
Authority for that, in the morose
Sense of the term. He was only

The son of a grocer, after all. I wanted
To be a cynic, *cum grano salis*,

As said by my Latin master. So I
Bought half the legal volumes on
Chancery Lane. It was all grist

To my mill: it was the sort
Of exploit I wanted, to make

A great tome of the Great Sessions
In Wales on the dissertations of
The Welsh Judges. In my study

At Brynoyre I also fashioned 'Old
Wales' before the bank at Brecon

Stopped it. I was always wearing
A black overcoat, obedient and green
With age, irritable when the glum

Children came up to thank Guy
Fawkes for his pennies. I took

My Army Lists to a Cambridge
College, but the Librarian mislaid
Them. When my wife complained after

My death that the Reverend Trevor
Williams at Aber Chapel was always

Preaching at her, she decided to go
To Llanfigan Church. I was
Not a great believer in sermons.

GWENFFREDA CATE WILLIAMS
ALICE MATILDA LANGLAND WILLIAMS
(ALIS MALLT)

When Kate Williams began her novelette
'Treverton Hall' she was fourteen. Alice
Was twelve. It was really the officers
From the camp at Slwch that fascinated
Them. Later it was India.

It was a word spoken by Gwenffreda
That made Mallt more refined, both
Of them daughters of 'Brychan', of
The ancient Irish line. They became
Novelists— 'The Dau

Wynne'— pronouncing their Welsh
Names in Aber Chapel with decorum,
With excited cries from the children
Who believed their flaunting robes
As if they were lords

And ladies. Fred was there too, but
Not in the other adventures. The girls
Were getting old, they felt, when
Taldir Jaffrennou and Fransez Vallée
Talked with them on

The canal while the Hon. Mrs Herbert,
'*La grande amie des Bretons*', was
Steering. In the evening Betsy Abadam
Sang with great abandon at Llanover.
It was not an easy

Thing to compose a poem in those
Halls and 'Abherve', as Fransez Vallée
Called himself, went back to Saint
Brieuc to collect himself. In 'The Two
Ways' Cate and

Mallt were supreme in the graces
Of Celtia. 'Playing the spark' did
Something for Breton voices too. It
Was two years later when 'A Maid
Of Cymru' was

Published. Perhaps it was Cate rather
Than Mallt who thought an Englishman
Would make 'Elor Meirch' his home. One
Cannot tell. At least it was not
The Dyffryn, anyway,

In its pages. But that was the end
Of the faded contents, for Cate died
Fourteen years later. Mallt persisted in
Going to Brittany and Ireland,
Always bountiful

With prizes and doing her Welsh
As she could. It was in Frederick's
House that she made her home in
The Towy valley, till limited means
Made her brother

Most unhappy. Could there be
Fortune for such a lady when
The last post was Plas Pontsaeson?
But that's not the reason for disquiet.
There was a place

That was sacred, the house of
Aberclydach, once the home of
John James Williams. Do you see
The tablets in the graveyard corner?
Shall it be to

Dismiss the *uchelwyr* as ever
Censorious? And for Mary Jane
Robertson Williams, should she
Turn back and, heart-whole, visit
Her father in

His costly estrangement. Who
Thinks of Brynoyre now? Does
William Retlaw Jefferson Williams
Think of it, despite his wife's pleas
From the hundred

And seventh psalm? Is there not
An answer, it may be, beyond
The vale of tears? Gwenffreda Cate
And Alis Mallt Williams have
Raised a token

Indiscretion. Were they not
Authoresses, Kinswomen to
All Celts, daughters of Brychan
In the Gorsedd of Britain? Did
They speak of poetry

And the watchword that many
Cowards would not put out? It
Was still a sad story, but the Celts
Were good at judging sad stories,
Don't you feel?

FREDERICK GEORGE ROBERTSON WILLIAMS

I was very good at timing the trains
To Talybont station, but especially if
Mabel Bridgewater, my Richmond friend,
Was due on the line. True, I was

Sometimes at Earl's Court or Paddington
When Mabel came on visits, when
Gwenffreda guested us, but I was not
The cheery partner Mabel would have

Me be. I wrote my diary, with its inked
Letters, sometimes at Aberclydach, often in
London. 'I Iʊ! I idd ılke ti os hwne
Hse iwnkde ta em', the girl from

The chorus in the Prince of Wales' Theatre.
But I was never brave, not even with
Mabel. Outside the Iron Church she patronised
Me, always talking of Richmond. I began

To think of my landowning interests, Berthlwyd
Fawr and Nantllanerch, that lack of prosperity
I had not foreseen, and so went up to Llanwrtyd
To find a bride. Nevertheless, I became

A rentier in the Teifi valley, dispirited,
Looking with anger at dogged obstacles.
Yet I was the last male of the family,
Believing how children might accomplish

Much if only the money lasted. Don't you
Remember me at Aberclydach, riding
My bike, looking to see if the trains are
Late? It was then I was a true spirit.

NOTES TO THE POEMS

Aber:
Aber, near Talybont-on-Usk, is where my mother's grave is situated.

Tŷ Clyd:
[1] Tŷ Clyd is the name of the house where my parents lived in the town of Brecon.
[2] Arafnah Thomas was once minister of the Plough Chapel.
[3] 'Two storeys of deed/Slapped on word' describes the conflict between my mother's independent, uncompromising pacifism with its rejection of organized 'established' religion and my father's position as a Congregational minister, formerly an army chaplain.

The Steward's Letter:
Alltyrynys is a mansion (still standing) in Walterstone, which is in the corner of Herefordshire adjoining Breconshire and Monmouthshire. From the thirteenth century it was the family seat of the Sitsillt family whose name subsequently became Cecil. The most famous member of that family, William Cecil, Lord Burghley, Secretary of State to Queen Elizabeth I, acquired the property in the 1590s when it passed to him from his cousin William, because of outstanding debt.

The poem is closely based on a letter written by Lord Burghley's steward in the area, Paul Delahay. The letter describes the funeral which he has organised for the deceased, William Cecil of Alltyrynys. William Cecil had nine children, of whom only one was a boy. Matthew, apparently 'unfitted in mind fᵣ preferment'. The second daughter was married to Paul Delahay.

Apparently, William Cecil had not led a blameless life, since Paul Delahay had to organize a lavish funeral to maintain the reputation and social standing of the family (and, by his family connection, of Lord Burghley himself).

William Cecil's first wife was Olive Parry whose brother is mentioned as being in the funeral procession. Maud Herbert, William's second wife, refused to come to the funeral. The funeral seems to have taken place over two days—a custom of Monmouthshire at the close of the sixteenth century.

The Path to Fontana Amorosa:
[1] The poem describes a walk to the Baths of Aphrodite in the far north-western corner of Cyprus. The walk takes the poet past the islet of Ayos Georgios.
[2] Ludovico Ariosto (1474-1533) was author of *Orlando Furioso* (1532), the greatest of the Italian romantic epics.
[3] Polis is a small town near the Turkish frontier in Cyprus. There is an inscribed tablet in Paphos dedicated to the parents of Onasias, once one of the inhabitants of Marion, a settlement which flourished some 2,500 years ago on the same site as the present town of Polis.

Innocent Dying:
Nant Iago is a stream which flows down from the former lead-mines of Mynydd Cedris. It joins the River Dysynni half a mile above Abergynolwyn.

Expiation:
[1] My grandfather was born in Llangattock and began trade as a builder in Cardiff before being advised for the sake of his health to move to the clearer air of the mountains to farm. This poem will be better understood if the poem 'Blue Blood and Englishmen' (*Snipe's Castle*, 1979) could be read first.
[2] 'Coedcae' is a rough piece of ground partly covered by trees and gorse bushes.
[3] Ffynnon Fawr was the farmhouse where I was born, near the Caerfanell stream (or Crafnell as it is now beginning to be known). The valley has since been flooded for a reservoir, and all that remains of Ffynnon Fawr are a few stones and a conifer near the edge of the reservoir.

They, Without Us:
[1] I was reminded of the poet 'Crwys', whom I knew as an old man (Williams Crwys Williams, 1875-1968).
[2] Baldwin, king of Jerusalem (died 1118), and Frederick Barbarossa of Germany (1121-90), took part in the Second and Third Crusades.
[3] Cynog was a sixth-century saint of Breconshire. Thomas Coke (1747-1814), born at Brecon, was a Methodist evangelist in Britain and America. Thomas Price ('Carnhuanawc') (1783-1848), another Breconshire man, was a Church of England cleric and a proponent of the Welsh language.

Roger Price (1834-1900), also a native of Breconshire, became a Congregational missionary in South Africa, and was known as the 'Lion of Bechuanaland'.

Cynog:
(From the Cott. MSS in the British Museum: Vespasian A. XIV. Of the Situation of Brecknock).

St. Cynog (fl. 500) was the son of Brychan Brycheiniog, the king of Brycheiniog (formerly Garthmadryn) after the death of his father Aulach. Drichan was tutor to both Brychan and his son Cynog.

Legend has it that Cynog had a decorated torque given to him by his father, and after Cynog's death the torque became a most precious relic. It has not survived, but Giraldus Cambrensis saw it and gave a detailed description.

Cynog's place of death is uncertain but the story is told that Irish raiders hurled him from the top of a cliff into one of two streams, the Yscir or the Yscir Fechan.

On Discovering Daumier's 'Don Quixote Reading' in the National Museum at Cardiff:
[1] Beltenebras was Amadis of Gaul, a fictional character in one of the prose romances written by the Portuguese Vasco of Loberia (died 1403)—and others—which made up fourteen books altogether.
[2] The Lord of Taprobane is thought to have been the overlord of Ceylon. Ptolemy in the second century AD and Isidor of Seville (c. 560-636) thought it was a Celtic country, part of the Summer Country where the Celts lived long before the northerners or the Persians came. It is often spelt 'Deffrobani'.

On South Lord's Land:
[1] On a mountain pasture near Dent, in Cumbria.
[2] See *Brigantia: A Mysteriography* by Guy Raglan Phillips (Routledge and Kegan Paul, 1976), which gives useful information about the legends of the kingdom of Brigantia (the area of present-day Yorkshire, Lancashire and Cumbria.)

The cult of the raven may long have persisted in the Rheged area of north-west Brigantia. In 'The Dream of Rhonabwy' from the Mabinogi, the Prince of Rheged, Owain ab Urien (though probably not of Arthur's vintage), is described as playing *gwyddbwyll* (a game like chess) with Arthur. Arthur's men attack Owain's ravens and Arthur ignores Owain's pleas, insisting that he must continue the game. The ravens then attack Arthur's men, but a truce is finally called. It would seem that Arthur's soldiers often kept an uneasy and untrusting peace with Rheged.

Ronan:
[1] The story of Ronan appears in *Légendes traditionelles de la Bretagne* by O. -L. Aubert.
[2] Ronan was an Irishman who received a call to go to the province of Cornouaille in Brittany, becoming a hermit in the highlands. Menez Hom is the highest hill in Brittany.

Grasshoppers:
The Rhinerhorn is a mountain south of Glaris, near Davos in Switzerland.

The Lamentation of Marchell:
The Lamentation of Marchell is part of the Account of Brychan of Brycheiniog (see Poem 11).

Marchell was the daughter of Tewdrig, king of Garthmadryn. Her father saw an alliance with the men of Dublin as a way of countering the influx of other Irishmen coming over the mountains. At her father's command, she was to cross to Ireland to marry Aulach of Dublin.

The Ui Liathain (Sons of Liathan) had already settled in the south of Glamorgan. Historically it is debatable which group from Ireland first settled in the area of the Black Mountains of Carmarthen and Brecon Beacons, the Ui Liathain or the men of Leinster (Dublin), or possibly even the Déisi, from the area of the Gower, whom Marchell had to repulse on her way to Porthmawr, near St David's, before embarking for Ireland.

The Clear Sea:
[1] From *The Voyage of St Brendan: Journey to the Promised Land*, translated from the Latin by John J. O'Meara: p. 21, 'The Clear Sea'.
[2] St Brendan was born around AD. 489 and died sometime between 570 and 583.

Look at me, Caleb:
The Holy Bible, Authorised King James Version, Numbers 13.

Half a dozen poems for the Spoon River Anthology after Edgar Lee Masters:
These poems are based on the lives of members of the Williams family of Aberclydach.

William Retlaw Jefferson Williams (1863-1944) was a historian and editor who, after his failure in his first case as a lawyer, retired to live for the rest of his life at Brynoyre near Talybont. He published four books on the parliamentary history of Wales and one on the history of the Great Sessions of Wales, all at his own cost. Between 1905 and 1907 he published the journal *Old Wales*, but his family inheritance was by then exhausted. He had to sell most of his valuable library to pay for his last great work, a full list of the officers of the British armed forces, but the manuscript was lost and never published.

Gwenffreda Cate and Alis Mallt, sisters of William Retlaw Jefferson Williams, were novelists who together wrote two novels under the pen-name of 'The Dau Wynne'. In 1899 the sisters met the Breton poets Abhervé (François Vallée) and Taldir (François Jaffrenou), and this inspired their lifelong interest in the Breton language. Alis Mallt, who lived long after her sister, was also a supporter of women's rights and one of the earliest and most generous supporters of Plaid Cymru.